Southern Comfort

Abandoned Homes of the American South

David Bulit

To my friends and family....

But most importantly Rusty.
Although you'll never read this because you're a cat.

CONTENTS

ACKNOWLEDGEMENTS

Many people helped with the creation of this book and I feel the need to thank them here.

Elizabeth A. "Bitsy" Gibson Wagner, for sharing the photos and history of her 1st cousin once removed, Leopold "Leo" Carl Simon.

Dagny Robertson, Secretary for Board of Directors of Dutton House Inc., for her help in some missing pieces of information regarding the Dutton House.

Nancy Stephens, who owned the Pendleton-Graves House between '89 and '93, for sharing her personal involvement and history with the home.

Rick and Mauriel Joslyn, President and Treasurer of the Sparta Historical Society, for sharing what photos and information they had on the Pendleton-Graves House.

John Daly of Green Gables at Historic Riverview Village, Inc. for the tour through the home and his extensive knowledge about the property.

And to all my friends and family who continue to support my work, especially those who travel and enjoy experiencing these places with me.

ARLINGTON

Located on the banks of the Mississippi River, Natchez is the county seat and only city in Adams County, Mississippi.

First established in 1716 by French colonists, Natchez was once a prominent city during the antebellum years as a center for cotton planters and trade on the Mississippi River. With the invention of the cotton gin in 1793 and high demand for cotton at the time with the growth of the textile industry in England, the advent of the steamboat which allowed transport northward on the river, and an already established population of slaves in the Deep South, Natchez was in a prime location.

The city attracted many Southern planters who grew crops of cotton and sugar cane using slave labor, exporting these crops upriver to northern cities and downriver to New Orleans. Many of these plantation owners built extravagant and elegant mansions, many of which still survive and serve as the city's backdrop today. Though many of these antebellum mansions have been preserved, one of these grand homes hasn't been so lucky.

Located on 55-acres in a wooded park, Arlington was built by John Hampton White, a native of Elizabethtown, New Jersey, and his wife, Jane Surget White. The actual year of Arlington's construction is unknown but it is widely believed the home was built sometime between 1816 and 1820.

According to the floor plan, this used to be the drawing room, the room to the right as you enter through the front door.

The land Arlington now stands on was first purchased in 1806 by Lewis Evans, who used the land to establish a plantation and built a house. In 1814, a portion of the land was sold to Jonathan Thompson, a land speculator. According to deed records, he owned the property until he sold it to Jane White in 1818, with the deed mentioning "extensive improvements". John Hampton White died on October 15, 1819 during a yellow fever epidemic. Jane White died on July 1, 1825.

Although there is no documentation, Arlington's design has long been attributed to Levi Weeks, the architect of the nearby Auburn antebellum mansion and many others in the area.

The floor plan consisted of a grand central hall that opened from the front door to the back, flanked by two rooms on each side, with a staircase located in a separate hallways located between two of the rooms. This same floor plan can be seen at other antebellum mansions in the area, most notably Rosalie (ca.1820) which is a near carbon-copy of Arlington.

One of the bedrooms with clear fire damage. The second consisted of four bedrooms and no bathrooms when it was first built.

In 1973, Arlington was listed on the National Register of Historic Places and due to its historical and national significance, it was further declared a national Historic Landmark in 1974. It is one of only 40 National Landmarks in the entire state of Mississippi, 12 of which are in Natchez.

On September 17, 2002, Arlington suffered major damage due to a fire which destroyed the roof and most of the second floor, including many of the early furnishings and art that were inside of the mansion.

Shortly thereafter, a new roof was built through the efforts of the Historic Natchez Foundation. Unfortunately, not much was done afterwards to protect the house as vandals broke out all of its windows and defaced much of the interior and exterior woodwork. The Natchez Preservation Committee cited the current owner, Dr. Thomas Vaughan of Jackson, Mississippi for demolition by neglect in July 2008.

Arlington was named the second most endangered historic property in Mississippi in 2009 by the Mississippi Heritage Trust who releases a top 10 endangered places list every year since 1999.

Later in December 2009, Dr. Vaughan was charged and found guilty of demolition by neglect, and ordered to pay just a $259 fine. During the court hearing, which Dr. Vaughan never bothered to show up to, Building Inspector Paul Dawes reviewed a timeline dating back to when Dr. Vaughan was first cited for demolition by neglect by the Natchez Preservation Committee.

Dawes and other city officials have failed to get in contact with Dr. Vaughan in the past about maintaining the historic property. Dawes also submitted a letter by Mayor Jake Middleton and the Natchez Board of Alderman citing Vaughan's failure to obey a public safety violation concerning high grass and weeds growing around the property.

Dawes submitted photos from February 2009 and December 2009 to illustrate how much the property had deteriorated in such a short amount of time.

He also talked about drug paraphernalia littered around the property, as well as a bulldozer, backhoe, a man lift, a bucket truck. There were also two dump trucks which he explained were inoperable as vandals had removed the radiators from them.

In 2012, Dr. Vaughan appeared in court once again due to not keeping the property up to code. Over the next two years, Vaughan was given a variety of fines including a citation in July 2013 which he pleaded guilty to in regards specifically to the overgrown lot.

Opposite: The stair hall situated in the center of the house.

It was first reported in August 2014 that Vaughan was looking into selling the property and was giving the judge overseeing his case continued updates on the upkeep of the property.

Just a few months later, Vaughan had decided he did not want to sell the home as it has been in his family for many years, but was working on improving the property by adding a gate at the driveway entrance and removing any graffiti from the walls. Despite this, the house is still very much in ruins and will remain in this condition for the foreseeable future.

Postcard depicting Arlington, circa 1930s

Opposite: The grand hall which used to be filled with suits of armor and paintings decorating the walls.

ASHLAR HALL

Robert Brinkley Snowden was born in Memphis, Tennessee, on March 9th, 1869, six weeks before his father, Colonel Robert Bogardus Snowden, purchased Annesdale mansion. His mother, Annie Overton Brinkley Snowden, was daughter of Colonel Robert C. Brinkley, one of the largest property owners in early Memphis and owner of the original Peabody Hotel in downtown Memphis. Annie Overton was also a granddaughter of Judge John Overton who, with General Andrew Jackson and James Winchester, laid out the town of Memphis in 1816.

Robert Brinkley Snowden received his early education at private schools in Memphis, studied at the University of South Sewanee, Tennessee In 1888 and graduated from Princeton in 1890 where he studied architecture.

Snowden, along with his various business partners, was known for developing three of Memphis' earliest subdivisions; Annesdale Park, Annesdale-Snowden, and Stonewall Place. Him and his partners were also known at the first developers to pay for streets, sidewalks, and other improvements in their subdivisions and then deed them to the city.

Snowden was also responsible for the construction of the Commerce Title Building, Chisca Hotel, Lowenstein Building, National Bank of Commerce, and the current Peabody Hotel, all of which are now Memphis historical landmarks.

During these years in Memphis, he lived in Ashlar Hall where he remained until his death in 1942. Built in 1896, the two-story mansion was designed by Snowden as a mock castle, and included eight rooms, a basement, and attic space which contained the servants' quarters. The ashlar stone, for which the mansion is named, was barged in from Indiana and set in place by masons from Nashville. The final cost of the construction of the mansion was $25,000, equivalent to about $725,000 today.

After his death, the mansion was passed on to his heirs and after upkeep was proven difficult for them, they applied with the city for non-residential use of the building. His wife, Sara Day Snowden, passed away in 1956 and Ashlar Hall and its seven acre property was purchased by Memphis investors in 1957 for $50,000 per acre.

High-rise apartment buildings were constructed to east and west of Ashlar Hall and for a moment was threatened with demolition before it was purchased and used as a restaurant.

Used to cover the roof, a blue tarp hangs off the side of the building, exposing it to the elements.

The interior has been vandalized throughout the years. You can see to the right where someone spray painted where a camera was located at.

The bedrooms were transformed into dining rooms and operated by the Grisanti family in the 1960s. By 1970, it was known as Ashlar Hall Restaurant and it was during this time that the front lawn was paved over for more parking spaces.

On January 13, 1983, Ashlar Hall was added to the National Register of Historic Places. The building continued to be run as a restaurant until the 1990s, when it was purchased by Robert Hodges, better known as Prince Mongo.

Mongo claims to be a 333-year-old alien ambassador from the planet Zambodia sent to Memphis by Zambodian spirits to protect the city from natural disasters. Often dressed in outlandish outfits, he usually wears steampunk goggles, a long blonde wig, a beaded headdress, and various other accessories usually incorporating rubber chickens in some way.

Since 1978, he has run for Mayor of Memphis every year, but never winning and usually garnering no more than 1% of the votes. He's also no stranger to the law as he's been arrested

a number of times, usually due to contempt of court. He made national news once in 1983, when he was sentenced to 10 days for contempt when he appeared in court wearing green body paint, a fur loincloth, gold goggles, and carrying a skull under one arm.

Mongo is also thought to be financially secure, owning a number of homes in Memphis, Virginia Beach and a $2 million mansion in Fort Lauderdale, complete with a yacht docked out on the water. No one really know where or how he gets his money, but some people have theorized that he inherited money from his family. There are also theories out there that say he might have an insurance or disability claim and continues to act insane to keep collecting money.

Lights, speakers, and an old television set are some of the things left behind when Mongo closed down the Castle.

Opposite: A piano sits underneath the staircase, a remnant from Ashlar Hall's club days.

First known to the public for Prince Mongo's Pizza in midtown Memphis, he moved on to bigger endeavors and opened Prince Mongo's Planet, a three-story and 30,000 square feet nightclub.

In the 1990s, he turned Ashlar Hall into the Castle which quickly became notorious due to allegations of serving alcohol to underage drinkers and for people skinny dipping in the club's pool. Police frequently visited the club due to noise complaints from neighbors, many who lived in the two high-rise buildings that sit adjacent to it.

In 1992, two underage girls were killed in a drunk driving accident after leaving the Castle. Mongo was able to avoid charges by owning the property, but then "gifting" the business to an employee, making him nothing more than a landlord. He claims to be innocent of any underage drinking accusations, pointing out that he has never even held a liquor license in his name.

At one point, the Fire Marshal changed the occupancy inside the Castle from 451 to 88. When he was found to be in violation of the new number of occupants allowed, he responded by dumping 800 tons of sand in the parking lot, moving patrons outside to party.

Once mounting fines and environmental court issues became too much to handle, Prince Mongo closed the Castle. He quit-claimed the property to Kenny Medlin, owner of the non-profit Urban Renaissance Initiative, who planned to find tenants for the building to offset the costs of the repairs needed.

The condition of the mansion worsened after signing a lease to George Keith Williamson Jr. to turn Ashlar Hall into a restaurant. While Medlin was in Chicago for a conference, Williamson removed portions of the roof, a significant amount of copper from the building exterior, and the large stone beams from the portico. Along with the original stonework, Medlin claimed that the restaurant equipment inside was stolen too.

An investigation was launched that found an arrest history

for Williamson, including theft of services and passing bad checks. Williamson was said to have skipped town after a warrant was issued for his arrest.

The latest owner, Juan Montoya, who moved to Memphis from Colombia in the early-2000s, is a contractor and real estate investor who purchased the building in 2016. He plans on restoring the building to its original state, but there are no plans on what the building will be used for.

The second floor of the mansion. Mongo had a unique chandelier installed in the middle here which was to portray the Earth falling, but it has since been removed along with everything else belonging to the nightclub.

TOURO-SHAKSPEARE HOME

Judah Touro was born on June 16, 1775, in New port, Rhode Island. His family moved to New York in 1780 after the British captured Newport, and then to Kingston, Jamaica in 1782. His father died a year later and his mother moved the family to Boston to live with her brother, Moses Michael Hays, a merchant and philanthropist who helped founded Boston's first bank. When his mother died in 1787, Judah and his siblings were raised by his uncle.

In October 1801, Judan moved to New Orleans, where he opened a small store selling soap, candles, codfish, and other exports from New England. He eventually became a prominent merchant and shipowner, particularly after the Louisiana Purchase in 1903, which caused a large growth of the region and its economy.

Unable to fight, Judah enlisted in Andrew Jackson's army in the War of 1812. In the Battle of New Orleans, he volunteered to carry ammunition to the batteries when he was struck in the thigh by a twelve-pound cannonball, tearing off a large chunk of flesh. Left for dead, he was saved by fellow merchant Rezin Davis Shepherd, who nursed Touro back to health and remained friends throughout their lives.

After the war, Touro continued building his business interests in trade, shipping, and real estate. He remarked that his fortune came from living a simple life instead of a lavish

Sketch of Judah Touro. *Laura Carter Holloway, published 1884*

one, as he lived in a small apartment and never his mortgaged properties to acquire new ones.

Touro was a philanthropist whose contributions are still remembered and honored to this day. In New Orleans, he opened an infirmary for sailors suffering from yellow fever and a synagogue, now the United States' oldest synagogue outside of the original thirteen colonies.

After his death in 1854, his bequeathed his $1 million estate to various causes, about $27 million in today's economy. One of his bequests was the establishment of an almshouse for the elderly poor in the city.

The Touro Almshouse was incorporated in 1855 and the executors of his estate acquired land donated by Rezin Davis Shepherd, Touro's lifelong friend. A towering Gothic structure, the building was designed by William Alfred Freret Jr. and completed in April 1862.

The front entrance to the Touro-Shakspeare Home. The spelling is a matter of small debate as its regularly spelled 'Shakespeare', even though it was partially named after former Mayor Joseph Shakspeare and is spelled Shakspeare along the front facade.

That same month, Union troops captured New Orleans without resistance and occupied the Touro Almshouse, filling it with gun racks, provisional beds and a kitchen. The almshouse would become the official headquarters for the native guards which included the Union Army's 1st Louisiana Native Guard, a fighting force of over 1,000 men composed mostly of African-American former slaves who had escaped to freedom.

After the Confederate surrender in April 1865, Union officials had planned to vacate the almshouse by September 1st, 1865, as it was no longer needed. On the last day of their occupancy, troops were cooking baked beans in the kitchen when sparks ignited combustible materials in the makeshift air duct they had used for the kitchen. The fire spread quickly as the tar roof ignited, and by morning, Touro's Gothic almshouse was in ruins.

The open courtyard situated in the middle of the building.

Due to public interest in Touro's first almshouse, a second building was constructed in 1895 in Uptown, funded through Mayor Joseph A. Shakspeare's gambling tax. As the area became more populated, the uptown site was subdivided into residences in 1927 and the facility was relocated to Algiers.

Named the Touro-Shakspeare Almshouse, the new building was built in 1933 and designed by William R. Burk, who was quoted in 1929 that his design "calls for a building that is as beautiful and dignified as a private residence, but which also bears the stamp of being a municipal building."

The building remained in operation for 72 years, serving as the city's almshouse and then as a senior care facility managed by Touro Shakspeare Inc., still owned by the City of New Orleans just as Touro envisioned it. Due to damages sustained during Hurricane Katrina in 2005, the Touro-Shakspeare Home was shuttered and would never reopen.

In 2009, Jahncke & Burns Architects was contracted with designing a restoration plan for the building. The contract was extended to include supervision of the construction, but the City of New Orleans ultimately abandoned the project, leaving the building in a state of ruin.

In 2016, the City successfully appealed to FEMA to draft a Section 106 Review in order to mothball the property. FEMA agreed that they would provide funding for the removal of lead paint, mold and asbestos, the removal of debris and non-historic building materials, and the installation of security measures. Despite this, the project has not begun and has no future commencement date.

Much of the interior is gutted, filled with trash, and any metal worth of value have been pulled out of the walls.

CAMP ALGIERS

Following the attack on Pearl Harbor in 1941, the Roosevelt administration authorized the United States to detain allegedly potentially dangerous enemy aliens, known as the Enemy Alien Control Program ran by the State Department. FBI and other agencies forced tens of thousands of Japanese, Italian and German Americans into internment camps, based solely on their ancestry.

According to Max Paul Friedman, a history professor at American University in Washington D.C., more than a million and a half German lived in Latin America at the time. Fearing that some may be Nazi agitators, saboteurs, or spies who could potentially rise up and begin a new front, the Roosevelt administration ordered FBI agents to Latin America, find anyone suspected of being a Nazi, and bring them back to the United States.

Due to the war though, the best and highly-trained agents were either overseas or busy with homeland security. So bottom-levels agents, who could not speak Spanish or German and weren't trained all too much, were sent to Latin America for this task.

Because they didn't have much talent, their methods were less than professional, and relied on simply paying locals to give up their German speaking neighbors. This opened a new

level of corruption as Latin American dictators would falsely accuse their own residents as Nazis and then seize their property.

At the time, it was illegal for the United States to seize individuals from outside the country. To get around this, Latin American deportees were forced to give up their paperwork to officials on the transport boats. When they arrived at the port of New Orleans without any papaerwork, were denied visas. Because of this, they were then arrested on the grounds that they tried to enter the country illegally and were subject to internment. Once arrested, they were shipped off to various internment camps across Oklahoma, Texas, and Georgia.

Because so many deportees were falsely accused, a large majority had no affiliation with the Nazi party. There were a decent number of people though once affiliated with the Nazi party throughout the camps. Because the United States was worried about the health and welfare of their own people imprisoned in Europe, they allowed these sympathizers to do as they pleased, be it flying the swastika flag, singing Nazi songs, or giving the Nazi salute.

Of these deportees, approximately 81 of them were Jewish. A small number of them had actually fled Europe seeking refuge in the United States, but were denied visas. So they went to Latin America instead where they were falsely accused of being Nazis, sent to United States and interned there with actual Nazis.

Jewish internees were discriminated against, and beaten in the camps. They demanded they be moved elsewhere, where they didn't have to fear for their lives at the hands of Nazis. Camp commanders followed by writing to Washington D.C., asking why they were housing and guarding whole families and the elderly, when they were supposed to be watching over dangerous Nazis.

Opposite: The interior of one of the homes, on the property of the former Camper Algiers.

A chalkboard is about the only thing left in the homes, though it's uncertain if it was originally part of the home or a remnant from where the Orleans Parish School Board owned the property.

Officials decided there would be a camp specifically to house those who opposed Nazis and their ideals. Camp Algiers in New Orleans was chosen as that camp and starting in 1942, most of the 81 Jewish internees and other innocent prisoners were relocated there. The camp would become known as the "camp for the innocents".

Residents of Camp Algiers had access to a library stocked with English, Spanish, and even a small number of German books. There was also a kitchen here where families enjoyed meals together, while single men ate separately from them. Residents were even ferried over to Canal Street where they could shop in the department stores there, and could even participate in the parades during Mardi Gras. Children were also allowed to go to school at nearby Algiers elementary and high schools.

There was some work done on them to potentially save them, but some of the houses are probably too far gone to save.

Due to pressure from local advocates and the National Refugee Service against the detention of Jews and urging their release, a decision was made in 1943 to release them on a few conditions.

They were sent to Detroit, Cincinnati, St. Louis, Philadelphia, Cleveland, and other large cities where they were watched over by an American foster family, and had to regularly report to an immigration officer. Essentially, they were on parole.

However, six Jews remained at Camp Algiers, in part because they were single males or because they could find someone to sponsor them if released. In 1944, a group of pro-Nazi Germans were sent to Camp Algiers and elected Kurt Ludecke, former advisor to Hitler, to head the internee committee. The "camp for the innocents" was no longer so innocent as interned Jews feared for their lives once again at the hands of Nazis.

After the war, many of the former internees remained in the United States. Most eventually made their way back home where they found that their property was gone or seized by the government, and had to go through a legal process to recover their property or start their lives from scratch.

Camp Algiers was decommissioned and a portion of it is now used by U.S. Customs and Border Protection. Another portion was used by the Orleans Parish School Board until 2005 when Katrina severely damaged the buildings on the property. These buildings, once officer quarters during the war, are either on the verge of collapse or have collapsed already.

The school board sold the property in 2011 to First NBC Community Development Fund, LLC, a subsidiary of First NBC Bank. First NBC Bank would later collapse in the spring of 2017, but not before offloading the property to another LLC.

There are a total of five homes left in varying states of ruin.

Opposite: Not pictured, the entire back portion of this home is missing.

AZALEA ORIGINAL PET CEMETERY

Grace Agnes Matt married John "Jack" Thompson, both 22 years old at the time, in Kansas City, Missouri. Six years later, they divorced after Grace has an affair with Arthur Wynne, running off with him to Oklahoma City where they marry in January 1920.

In 1924, Grace gave birth to her daughter, Dorothy. Allegedly being Arthur's child, Dorothy grew up calling Jack Thompson "Daddy Jack", and used the Thompson name as an adult. Despite having remarried as well to Mary L. Thompson, Jack visited Grace often in Oklahoma City.

Grace divorced Arthur in 1931 and moved back to Kansas City with Dorothy where according to a court testimony, Jack had become "an influential politician, a successful operator of slot machines and a man of considerable means." Jack was supposedly one of the top men in Tom Pendergast's organization, a political boss who controlled Kansas City and Jackson County, Missouri, who was known for rigging elections, paying off police, running gambling houses, and smuggling alcohol during the Prohibition-era.

While in Kansas City, Grace lived at the Pickwick Hotel, with Jack paying the bills and showering her with money and gifts.

Jealous of Mary Thompson and wanting Jack all to herself, Grace waited in the shadows outside of their home in Kansas City. On September 13, 1934, Mary and Jack were returning from vacation when Grace ambushed her, shooting her five times with a .25-caliber pistol. A witness later testified in court that Grace was calm after the murder, saying, "You don't have to hold me. I am not going to run away. It is all fixed. They won't do anything to me."

Grace was declared insane and was committed to a lunatic asylum in St. Joseph, Missouri. Just six months later, as doctors were ready to deem her fit to stand trial, Grace was allowed a leave of absence to visit her mother at in hotel in town. She then fled to New Orleans with her mother and Dorothy.

On December 3, 1935, Jack Thompson arrived in New Orleans to meet with Grace, but died that night in the Jung Hotel on Canal Street. Though it was ruled a heart attack, many found it very suspicious. Grace claimed to have never met Jack that evening and that he was killed for his "hidden fortune" of $400,000 to $500,000, which was reportedly never found.

The following day, Kansas City authorities asked New Orleans police and the public to be on the lookout Grace Wynne, who was hiding out somewhere in the city, except she wasn't hiding at all. Grace had opened up the Cottage Flower Shop, and became an organist at the Our Lady of Lourdes Church, where she composed a number of hymns and published a book in 1939.

The hymn book was used by church organists throughout the world and would later lead to her arrest. On July 27, 1940, Kansas City tracked Grace down due to the book she published and arrested her at her flower shop.

Louisiana Governor Sam Jones ordered for Grace's extradition to Kansas City and in 1942, was convicted for second-degree murder and sentenced to 15 years in prison. On September 5, 1944, The Missouri Supreme Court ordered a

Open tombs at the abandoned pet cemetery, estimated to have 5,000 pets buried on the property.

retrial due to a technicality, scheduling the trial for the following month. Grace was released on bail and fled once again to New Orleans.

During an extradition hearing in 1945 in front Louisiana Governor Jimmie H. Davis, Grave and her attorneys argued that enemies of Tom Pendergast were the ones pushing for her extradition back to Kansas City, that they weren't really interested in the murder charge and instead, wanted to know the location of Jack's hidden fortune. Davis denied the extradition request.

By 1946, Grace, her mother, and Dorothy had moved to the Toca Plantation located in on the banks of Bayou Terre aux Bouefs, a channel of the Mississippi River in St. Bernard Parish.

Back in March 22, 1845, plantation owner Phillipe Toca faced off in a duel with his rival, Gilbert Leonard. Standing 50 yards apart, each loaded their guns with a single bullet and fired, but only Toca's shot landed, killing Leonard on the spot.

A gravestone sticks out of a tree's roots, which reads "In loving memory of General Yen."

This killing was appropriate considering the deaths that would soon follow Grace and her family.

By the time they moved there, Toca Plantation was nothing more than an abandoned sugar cane field with a large Edwardian house at its center, built in 1909 by St. Bernard Sheriff Albert Estopinal Jr. Dorothy later recalled that her mother "had the idea of a pet cemetery in the back of her mind ever since a dog of which she was very fond died in Kansas City, and there was no place of burial there." The sugar cane field was converted into a pet cemetery and by 1952, Grace was running it full-time.

It was referred to as the E.E. Matt Cemetery, after Grace's mother Emma Matt, and the Azalea Original Pet Cemetery, for the 12-foot azalea trees which grew alongside the tombstones. There are an estimated 5,000 pets buried in the cemetery, mostly cats and dogs, but also parrots, rabbits, monkeys, hens, at least one cheetah, and a boa constrictor named Serita that performed on the "The Tonight Show" the in 1960s.

On November 26, 1970, Dorothy fatally shot first husband, Logan Banks, in the rear of the cemetery. According to the police report, Dorothy claimed Banks was intoxicated and threatening to kill them with a large knife. St. Bernard Sheriff's officials determined the killing was in self-defense and no charges were filed.

In 1976, Dorothy married her second husband, Donald Robinson, a caretaker on the property. Less than two years later, Robinson was fatally shot at the cemetery. Dorothy called police and told them she had found him dead. Again, no charges were filed.

Grace Wynne died of natural causes in August 1979 at the age of 88. A few months after her mother's death, Dorothy hired Brandon Nodier to do home repairs and as a live-in caretaker.

A human-sized Buddha Statue, now broken in half, sits upon the grave of a pet cat.

A gravestone reads "Gretchen Wills", with rabbit droppings along the edge.

Brandon Nodier has had some troublesome times throughout his life. In 1961 at the age of 7, Nodier witnessed a former mental patient shoot his father three times in the head as his father slept. At the age of 18, he was convicted of burglary in New Orleans and sentenced to five years of probation. By the time he met Dorothy, Nodier was known as a con artist and a swindler to those living in the area.

Dorothy fell into a stupor after her mother's death and admitted to having a substance abuse problem later in life. In 1981, she signed over a 99-year lease with Nodier through his company, Brandon Renovations Inc., for a mere $20 a month.

In 1984, Brandon and his ex-wife Bonnie, fooled Dorothy into signing over the cemetery to them for $20,000. Later that year, Dorothy filed a lawsuit against Brandon and Bonnie alleging she was tricked into signing the sale papers.

Opposite: Tombstones varied in shape and size, from simple plaques to elaborate statues.

The pretrial was scheduled for April 26, 1985, but Dorothy went missing on April 13th. On May 2nd, her partially nude body was found by fisherman, miles away from the cemetery in the Mississippi River, wrapped in heavy steel chains and a garbage bag tied around her head. Police determined that she was killed in her house at the cemetery and then dumped in the river.

In November 1988, the lawsuit was resolved with the judge ruling that Dorothy's heirs own the pet cemetery property. Patricia Newman, who had been friends with Dorothy since 1980, became executor of her estate.

Always suspecting Brandon Nodier was the one who killed Dorothy, police could not find enough evidence to build a case against him. The case went cold until around 2009, when witnesses began coming forward with information on Nodier in accordance with Dorothy's death. According to police, witnesses spoke of nightmares and seeing Thompson's ghost, the guilt pushing them to come forward.

The remains of the 1909 Edwardian manor. Police determined Dorothy was killed here, and then her body was dumped in the Mississippi River.

Nodier surrendered to the St. Bernard Sheriff's Office on October 17, 2012. At the time of his arrest, officials said Nodier's record included burglary, drug charges, aggravated assault, and multiple illegal weapon charges. Witnesses who came forward also linked Nodier to other killings in New Orleans.

The pet cemetery is still there, abandoned and overgrown. Patricia Newman had tried selling the property for years, but no one is willing to clean it up fearing tombstones hiding in the weeds would ruin their lawn equipment or that graves had opened up due to Hurricane Katrina.

Police are often called to the cemetery to chase off kids who were drinking, doing drugs, or simply just hanging out. Treasure hunters are a regular sight as well, walking the grounds with metal detectors hoping to find Jack's hidden fortune, rumored to have been buried there by Grace long ago.

A gravestone reads, "Buttercat. My Friend. Dorothy Thompson, 1983." Dorothy would be murdered by Brandon Nodier 2 years later in her home.

NOLAN PLANTATION

Located in Bostwick, a small town with a population of just 365, the Nolan Plantation House was built in 1906 by James A. Nolan. This is actually the Nolan's family second home, with their first home still located in the area but is not accessible to photographers.

The Nolan farm operated from 1856 to about 1970 and covered around 2000 acres. Behind this house, to the west was a complex of farm structures and tenant homes. The store across the street was actually the commissary. Like most true plantations of its era, the Nolan property supported its own commissary, which was essentially a credit-based store for employees. Even today, there are still remnants of the family name and the impact they had on the area, ie. Nolan Store Road and Nolan Lake.

The house is currently owned by an individual who lives in Dacula, a small city just outside of Atlanta. He acquired the property in 1977 from James A. Nolan, not the same that built the house but a descendant, for just $16,800. Supposedly, it has been used in some filming sometime in the past two decades, including a FOX network series. That would explain the limited fixing up that has been done.

This is the second Nolan home, the first being located across the street.

Opposite: Carvings on the wall dating back to the 1990s.

You can make out the cracks in the wall from so many years of neglect.

FOSTER-THOMASON-MILLER HOUSE

Incorporated on December 12, 1809, the town of Madison was described in an early 19th-century issue of White's Statistics of Georgia as "the most cultured and aristocratic town on the stagecoach route from Charleston to New Orleans." Madison boasts a large number of antebellum and Victorian buildings and today, has one of the largest historic districts in the state of Georgia.

By 1850, Madison was established as an important educational center in the region, and around this time, two institutions were founded for higher education of young women. One of these was the Georgia Female College, first founded in 1849 and incorporated by an act of the Georgia Legislature in 1850. Since its opening, the Georgia Female College served as a cultural marker for the town of Madison, hosting important town events and having libraries which were accessible to the public.

Madison's growth and prosperity was interrupted, like many towns in the South, by the start of the Civil War in 1861. As a result of the war, the Georgia Female College was shut down in 1862.

After the war, there was an attempt to revive the college and students began to return after 1873, but enrollment never reached its pre-war figures. When the school building burned in 1881, the college was disbanded.

During the era, the entry hall was usually so grand to make a good first impression for visitors.

In 1883, the property was auctioned off and sold to Legare H. Foster who immediately commenced construction of his house of the site. The exterior foundation of the house was laid directly on top of the old foundation of the former college.

The Foster-Thomason-Miller House was built on the grounds of the former Georgia Female College. After serving as an important cultural marker for the town of Madison, the school was shut down in 1862 as a result of the war.

An article in the December 1, 1883 issue of the Madisonian Newspaper described Foster's newly constructed home as follows:

"Perhaps the most elegant country home in Middle Georgia is that of Legare H. Foster, in this city. Of all the attractive residences in Madison, this is the most desirable. A stranger to parsimony, this thrifty and comfort-loving gentleman has just completed, by contract, one of the most beautiful and costly residences ever built in this city. Daniel Townes, the contractor, a Madison mechanic, drew the plans and constructed the house. Every piece of work shows superior mechanical genius, and this edifice will for years be a monument to his skill and ingenuity. We hazard nothing of truth when we say that the most experienced contractor in any of the large cities in our State, could not excel the work which was just completed.

The residence is a beautiful frame building, situated on the old college lot on S. Main Street, with a dense shade of large live oaks in front. The front veranda is beautiful and novel in shape, there being a two-story bay window directly in front, making a desirable entrance to the lower hall, and a good ventilation to the upper. The two front rooms, parlor and drawing room, have side bay windows, and are elegantly decorated with frescoed walls, walnut and hardwood facings. The large folding doors are of solid walnut, and slide with ease which careful workmanship only can secure. The dining room is very elaborately finished with natural woods, as is the whole first floor —the blinds, the facings and wains-cotings being of ash and walnut. This room is beautifully frescoed by the artistic brushes of Sheridan Brothers, Atlanta. The staircase is a model of costliness and symmetry. The railing and facing are solid walnut.

The "red room" on the second floor, is one of the prettiest rooms we ever saw, and is finished at great cost—being beautifully frescoed. The "walnut room" and "oak room", the two rear rooms on the second floor, are beautifully finished in appropriate styles. We understand that Mrs. Foster will furnish these rooms with furniture adapted to correspond. The entire house will be lighted with gas. To sum it up, it is beautifully planned, handsomely finished, and does great credit to the skill of the contractor Townes, show up the enterprise of Mr. Foster—besides being an attractive acquisition to that part of the city. We congratulate our friend upon the completion of his home, and wish for him and his admirable wife all the happiness that can possibly bless two loving hearts."

The "red room", located on the second floor at the end of the hall, was described as the prettiest ever seen by the Madisonian Newspaper in 1883.

In 1889, the Fosters sold the house to Robert Usher Thomason, and over the next 90 years, three generations of the Thomason family would occupy the home. The exterior was repainted in 1905, and indoor plumbing and electricity was added in 1916.

In 1978, Richard and Marcia Miller purchased the home from the Thomasons and meticulously restored it, earning the Georgia Trust for Historic preservation award for residential restoration in 1986, the only home in Madison to earn such an award.

In 2001, a fire broke out in the back of the house, severely damaging a rear addition to the house. Although the fire didn't spread to the rest of the house, there was still significant smoke and water damage throughout the building.

Opposite: The parlor room usually was the formal room in the house and was usually used for entertaining guests.

The property was sold to new owners in 2009, but no visible efforts have been undertaken to stabilize or restore the structure. A developer had proposed plans to build additional houses on the eight acres behind the home. While the Foster-Thomason-Miller house is poised to not be disturbed due to those plans, its rehabilitation is also not included in those plans.

The Foster-Thomason-Miller house was listed on the Georgia Trust for Historic Preservation "Top 10 Places in Peril" for 2018; an annual listing that brings awareness to imperiled historic resources throughout the State.

The stairwell was constructed from solid walnut, and leads up to the second floor to the bedrooms.

The "walnut room". The fireplace is made of faux marble and encaustic tiles.

According to the floor plan, this was the "blue room", though now it's pink.

POMEGRANATE HALL

Pomegranate Hall was built in the 1830s by Nathan Sayre. Sayre moved from New Jersey to Sparta, Georgia in the early 1830s where he became a state attorney, a member of the Georgia legislature, and a superior court judge.

Although he never married, he had several children with one of his slave women and later lived with his common law wife, Susan Hunt, who was part Cherokee, African and white. It is believed the complicated layout of the home reflected on the equally complicated family dynamics. In his library at Pomegranate Hall, he was also known to keep books which argued against the common belief that the mixing of races would eventually produce inferior or degenerate children.

Pomegranate Hall was commonly referred to as the "half house". No one really knows why. One theory is that the much of the house was brought over by ship in the 1830s and then completed in Sparta, leaving the other half of the house in England. Another theory behind the name was due to the front door being located on the left side of the house rather than the center.

At the time, Pomegranate Hall was painted a "monastic brown" which gave it a Mediterranean appearance, and stood on several acres of land containing vineyards and Pomegranate trees which Sayre used to make his own wine.

The mansion was constructed of local stone and brick with walls two feet thick. Along the front of the house were 24 foot high columns. The back of the mansion was a whole three stories high, and was where it was said Sayre kept the family he had with his slave. The main floor contained an elaborate entrance hall, two reception rooms on the right, and Sayre's extensive library.

A guest at the house in 1839 described her upstairs room as "delightfully situated; our windows attracted all the breezes and commanded imposing and beautiful views of the whole town and surrounding country".

After Nathan Sayre's death in 1853, the house was bought by the Simpson family who owned it when writer Eliza Frances Andrews stayed there during the Savanah Campaign, better known as 'Sherman's March to the Sea'. She describes her experience on her way to Sparta in her book, The War-Time Journal of a Georgia Girl, 1864-1865:

"About three miles from Sparta we struck the "Burnt Country," as it is well named by the natives, and then I could better understand the wrath and desperation of these poor people. I almost felt as if I should like to hang a Yankee myself. There was hardly a fence left standing all the way from Sparta to Gordon. The fields were trampled down and the road was lined with carcasses of horses, hogs, and cattle that the invaders, unable either to consume or to carry away with them, had wantonly shot down to starve out the people and prevent them from making their crops. The stench in some places was unbearable; every few hundred yards we had to hold our noses or stop them with the cologne Mrs. Elzey had given us, and it proved a great boon. The dwellings that were standing all showed signs of pillage, and on every plantation we saw the charred remains of the gin-house and packing-screw, while here and there, lone chimney-stacks, "Sherman's Sentinels," told of homes laid in ashes."

The house then went to Seaborn Reese, a Representative from Georgia. Reese was born in Madison, Georgia in 1846. He attended the University of Georgia and after gaining admittance to the state bar in 1971, he began practicing law. From there, he moved to Augusta before finally settling in Sparta.

Reese was elected to the Georgia House of Representatives in the State General Assembly and served in that role between 1872 and 1874. From 1877 to 1880, Reese was the solicitor general of Georgia's northern judicial circuit. In 1982, he replaced Alexander Stephens in the United States House of Representatives during the 47th United States Congress, and was reelected in the 48th and 49th Congresses, serving until 1887. He served as judge of the northern judicial circuit between 1893 and 1900.

Reese died in Sparta on March 1, 1907, and was buried in the city's Methodist Church Cemetery.

In 1963, the widow of Oliver Macy, of the Macy's Department Store family, moved in and lived in Pomegranate Hall until she died in 1992.

The next owner was Emily Karolyn Hair, widow of the late historian Dr. William Ivy Hair.

On July 5th, 2001 the home heavily damaged due to a fire which destroyed much of the upper floor and roof. One online source stated that the house burned in 1990, but this was the time when Oliver Mary occupied the home. Other sources claim the blaze happened sometime between 1999 and 2000, but a newspaper clipping confirms it occurred in 2001.

According to locals, the fire was set by "accident" by Emily Hair, who was burning a pile of her son's clothes on his bed because he had a sever drug addiction and this was her way of coping with it. The fire spread quickly, traveling down the stairwell and into the furnace room, and then finally engulfing the entire second floor.

The home was bought by Jerry Erickson in 2005 from Steve Hair, who inherited the home from his late mother. After years of attempting to restore or at the very least, protect the home from the elements, funds had run out.

PENDLETON-GRAVES HOUSE

Just down the street from Pomegranate Hall is another house worth mentioning. Commonly referred to as the Pendleton-Graves House, it was built in 1815 by Thomas Whaley in the Plantation Plain style or I-house, an architecture style which is quite common throughout the Southern United States and described as being two rooms wide and one room deep.

In 1853, the home was purchased by Edmund Monroe Pendleton, who expanded the home to accommodate his large family. Grandnephew of 1st Chief Justice of Virginia Edmund Pendleton, he was born in Eatonton, Georgia in 1815. He began his formal education in local private schools but left after only a few years due to his family's financial misfortunes.

Pendleton went on to co-own a jewelry store in Columbus, and then later ran a business with his cousin in Macon. Here, he found a chemistry textbook which was his introduction to science and developed an interest in medicine. He began studying in the office of a local doctor and then became an apprentice to a local pharmacist.

In 1833, he enrolled in the Medical College of South Carolina in Charleston and graduated in 1837. He moved to Sparta where he practiced his profession where he became prominent in the development of agriculture and agricultural science in the South.

By the amount of garbage inside the home, it has probably been used by a number of homeless people throughout the years.

He developed the Pendleton formula for the manufacturing of fertilizer and what we still use today, and was the first to use animal matter as plant food. Along with his son, William Micajah Pendleton, they were the first to grind down cotton seed cake into meal and use it as an ingredient in the manufacture of fertilizers. Pendleton was also the first to observe that phosphoric acid and nitrogen were exhausted from the soil by cereal and cotton cultures.

Pendleton became a professor at the University of Georgia where he authored Scientific Agriculture with Practical Deductions, a textbook used extensively by colleges and schools.

He died on January 26, 1884 and is buried at the historic Oakland Cemetery located in the center of Atlanta.

Opposite: The main hall. The wood is a mix of cherry, oak, and walnut.

A sleeping bag and a large number of used candles sit on the floor, no doubt where someone had once been squatting.

In 1880, the home was purchased by Richard Augustus Graves, who expanded the house and gave it its Victorian appearance.

Graves moved to Sparta from Augusta and engaged in mercantile business, before opening the town's first commercial bank in 1887. The Bank of R.A. Graves moved to another building located on Broad Street in 1889, which still stands today. A couple of years later, he would go on to start Sparta's first real estate agency.

He held the office of Vice President of the Georgia Bankers' Association on several occasions and at the time of his death, was chairman of the Hancock County commission.

On December 27, 1901, Graves died in his home and was buried at Sparta Cemetery. At the time of his death, an article in the Atlanta Constitution described him as "a man of large wealth and prominence and was one of the best known and popular men in the county".

The house was purchased in 1989 by Nancy Stephens from

the attorneys handling the Graves estate for $30,000, including the Graves barn next door. According to her, the Pendleton-Graves house was vacant for 15 years before she bought it and folks in town were complaining about the condition of house.

According to her, it was full of lizards, king snakes, and ticks when she first moved in, who promptly caught Rocky Mountain spotted fever and was bedridden for the next 6 weeks.

Stephens removed the old calcimine paint and repainted the exterior and most of the interior of the house. Along with a new coat of paint, a new roof was added in 1992, fixing the leaks it had at the time. During the restoration work, she also found old letters from Pendleton behind the walls dating back to 1934.

After her retirement in 1993, the house was sold and since then, it has changed hands plenty of times without any of the owners doing any further restoration work, leaving the property in disrepair.

A postcard for the home of Mrs. Richard Augustus Graves, postmarked 1913. *Courtesy of the Sparta-Hancock County Historical Society*

BIRDSONG HOUSE

Just on the outskirts of Sparta is the unincorporated community of Mayfield, which consists mostly of middle to low class citizens. Back in the early 1800s though, Mayfield and all of Hancock County was thriving as plantations flourished due to the large demand for cotton.

Like the town of Madison, this growth was interrupted by the Civil War, the difference being that Hancock County never recovered after the war. The majority of the population in Hancock County at the time was mostly slaves, and much of the labor in the fields was also done by slaves. With no more slave labor, this forced many wealthy plantation owners to leave the county.

Cotton made resurgence in the late-1800s until the boll weevil hit the area in the 1920s, and cotton fields were abandoned once again.

Many plantation homes from this era still stand today, though one home in particular is worth noting that locals refer to as the Birdsong House. The Birdsong family were some of the earliest settlers in Hancock County, many of whom were prominent members of the community.

In the early-1930s, it was bought by Claude and Ruby Hill, who was a USPS carrier and ran a mercantile store respectively. They lived in the home with their children and

The main hall, painted pink with pink and baby blue wallpaper.

grandchildren until 1957, when the house was sold and they moved to Thomson.

Following the Hill and Elliot families, it was owned by Thomas Benjamin Rushing and his wife, Irene Rushing. They also owned the nearby corner store, now also abandoned, and cooked barbeque there on the weekends. In the late-1960s, he and his family also moved to Thomson and sold the home to John McCown.

John McCown was born on November 18th, 1934, in the Peedee region of South Carolina, just Northwest of Myrtle Beach. His father died in a traffic accident when John was just three years old. Not able to support her family, his mother moved to Harlem for better work opportunities and John moved in with his grandparents.

Growing up in the segregation era, McCown attended the all black Loris Training School where he would join the basketball team and eventually become class president. Feeling homesick, it wasn't long before he moved to Harlem to be with his mother.

Desks, chairs and paperwork were found in this portion of the home, likely used as a classroom in later years.

Being from the South, he found that the education system was much tougher in the North and struggled in school due to it.

McCown decided to join the Air Force and moved to Colorado. While stationed in Colorado Springs, he organized the city's first civil rights demonstration following the 16th Street Baptist Church bombing in Birmingham, Alabama, where four young black girls were killed and 22 others were injured.

Considered courageous and outspoken about his opinions, he gained favor with the local National Association for the Advancement of Colored People (NAACP) and was appointed military advisory to Edward Bradford, president of the Colorado Springs chapter. Throughout the 60s, he advocated for the abolishment of military bias towards blacks throughout the country.

After serving nearly ten years in the Air Force, he received a general discharge and made his way South to join Dr. Martin

Luther King Jr. and the Southern Christian Leadership Conference (SCLC) in Selma, Alabama, where massive marches were being organized due to voting restrictions placed on black Americans.

While in Alabama, McCown also befriended Stokely Carmichael, who believed less in nonviolence and interracial alliances, and more on black militancy. Carmichael would go on to coin the term "black power" and help rural African-Americans outside of Selma to form the Lowndes County Freedom Organization, an all-black, independent political group that became known as the Black Panther Party.

McCown would eventually rely on strong arm and intimidation tactics. While traveling throughout the South, he became involved in multiple rallies and protests, and would later brag that he was the one who pushed Mayor Ivan Allen off the car during the Atlanta riots in 1966.

He would go on to be selected executive director of the Georgia Council on Human Relations (GCHR), a non-profit and biracial organization working against prejudice and discrimination due to race, religion, ethnicity, and nationality.

He eventually made his way to Hancock County, regarded as one of the more tolerable communities towards blacks. The Ku Klux Klan never had an influence in the county as the film Birth of the Nation, a movie that portrayed blacks as unintelligent and aggressive towards white women and the Ku Klux Klan as heroic, never played in the county's only movie theater. Hancock County would become the only county in Georgia without a lynching.

Despite this and the passage of the Civil Rights Act of 1964 and the Voter Rights Act of 1965, schools, restaurants and water fountains were still segregated. White county leaders would also vote against any improvements that benefitted the black community.

Opposite: Cobwebs hang from the window and pieces of cardboard cover holes in the floor.

A large portion of the second floor is deteriorating due to leaks in the roof.

McCown decided that the only way change could occur, the black community need to be more involved in the political process, but there needed to be a black majority on the county commission.

In 1972, his idea was realized when he helped elect blacks into fourteen of the county's eighteen posts. It was also the first time Hancock County had a black majority in control of the school board.

He founded the East Central Committee for Opportunity (ECCO), and was able to bring in funds from both private and federal entities into the county. He also began investigating into why the Federal Housing Administration (FHA) was granting loans to such a low number of black residents. The investigation found a bias towards blacks, changes were made, and Hancock black residents began receiving housing loans.

Opposite: A closer look at the staircase in the main hall.

Over the next few years, Hancock County saw a large sum of grant money flow into it. Through ECCO, McCown constructed a 150-unit low-income housing development and a catfish farm which was described by TIME magazine as "one of the largest and most scientific catfish farms in the world". ECCO would later purchase large tracts of lands which included a cement block factory, control of the county hospital, and the only movie theater in the county.

The white citizens of Hancock County were fearful of McCown, feeling he was too powerful of a figure especially for such a small town. Fear escalated with reports of gunfire throughout the countryside and repeated threats by black citizens toward the all-white police force. In 1971, Mayor Buck Patterson purchased ten sub-machineguns for the six man police force. McCown responded by purchasing thirty sub machineguns and creating pamphlets advertising the "Hancock Sporting Rangers" as a "hunting club" and encouraged people to purchased shotguns and rifles.

Presumably, this is the dining room with the kitchen located in the back of the house.

This arms race ended when former Governor Jimmy Carter traveled to Sparta to serve as mediator between the two parties, leading two both sides giving up their sub machineguns.

Jeff Nesmith of the Atlanta Constitution wrote an article titled, "Nightclub Getting Hancock Poverty Funds," about grant money given to ECCO used to fund a nightclub and two airplanes at the international airstrip in Mayfield, which McCown also developed with the use of federal funding. This article also brought up the question as to why such a small town needs an international airstrip, especially when half of its residents are living in poverty. As Nesmith would later write:

"In 1966 John McCown came to this sleepy town in poverty-ridden Hancock County as a black civil rights worker, supported by a wage that proved just enough to live on. Today he owns 525 acres of Hancock County farmland, is building a house that will cost nearly $60,000, holds the title to several pieces of commercial property in Sparta and flies his own twin-engine airplane, price tag $33,000. How in eight years a hungry black civil rights worker could become that prosperous in a rural Georgia county where poverty and racism have maintained an iron grip since the Civil War has become a question a lot of people want answered."

In 1971, McCown was questioned by members of the GCHR on some financial inconsistencies, followed by his resignation as executive director. Accounts were audited and found some questionable land deals which resulted in an undocumented $50,000 for ECCO, and a loss of over $290,000 in the catfish farm with over $120,000 paid toward travel and consultant fees.

In the summer of 1974, McCown was jailed for unlawful assembly, failure to disperse and obstruction of a police officer. With McCown jail, violence swept through Sparta as 600 protestors converged on the jail. During this time, there were also two shotgun attacks; one at the home of a former policeman and one at a store owned by the brother of Police Chief Garrett.

The fireplaces in the home have since been bricked up, with pipes which used to be connected to the boiler for heating.

McCown would later lead a march through downtown Sparta to the Sparta Baptist Church. Armed with guns, they forced the members of the congregation out, barricaded the doors, and held their own service. Following the service, they left the church and lay in the middle of the highway blocking all traffic.

McCown would later tell a reporter from the Augusta Chronicle, "I'm not a violent man but if someone stands in my way, I believe I should kill them." He would follow that up when, standing with pistols in his belt shouted to television cameras, "I'll destroy the town of Sparta, I don't give a damn about whites."

A subsequent investigation found that McCown had brought in over $8.7 million in grant money in Hancock County. Much of it was squandered off due to poor planning, mismanagement, and over spending.

A bedroom on the second floor, a bouquet of fake roses sits on a chair near the window.

With the ongoing investigation, the Ford Foundation which provided grants to ECCO announced they would no longer be funding them. When attempting to post bail for two members of his group, McCown found that he had a negative net worth. A few months later on January 31, 1976 all employees of ECCO were terminated as the Office of Economic Opportunity, which also provided grants to ECCO, had run out of money.

The night before on January 30, 1976, after receiving news that funding had run out, McCown spent the night drinking with friends at the ECCO owned night club. Deciding to go for a quick flight, McCown drove the three men to Cessna 182 single engine plane. Not owning a pilot's license, he simply took off.

Within minutes from takeoff, the planes plunged into the pine forest, killing McCown and two of the men; the third man was thrown out of the plane and was found alive. McCown was found to have a blood alcohol level of 0.198, nearly twice the legal limit to drive a car in Georgia. The National

Transportation Safety Board also found no malfunctions or and mechanical failures in the plane.

Questions were raised as to how McCown came into ownership of the aircraft. The plane was found to have been registered to a black college in Mississippi, which had given McCown an honorary degree. Logs showed the aircraft was donated to the college and no connections to McCown were found.

Regardless of McCown's death, the investigation into ECCO continued. Over a dozen individuals were indicted, all of whom pleaded down and served minimal sentences, returning to their government jobs within the county.

ECCO owned many businesses and properties, including a hospital facility, a wood products manufacturing operation, a metal fabricating plant, a clothing store that offered children's apparel, and a local bank which funded small business-ventures, all of which were shut down. The catfish farm which was highly praised at the time of its construction was nothing more but dried up ponds.

By 1977, the once bustling town of Mayfield now resembled a ghost town. John McCown is buried behind the Birdsong house in Mayfield, his grave now tended to by locals. The house is currently abandoned and is planned to be torn down in the future.

Opposite: John McCown's grave behind his old home in Mayfield.

J.C. LITTLE HOUSE

James Cain Little was born in Jefferson County, Georgia to Robert Patterson Little and Elizabeth Cain Little on February 7, 1846. Robert P. Little was a successful and influential plantation owner and served in the state legislature for two terms.

J.C. Little attended school until August 4th, 1863, when he enlisted in the Confederate Army at the age of seventeen. He joined as a private in Company F, 8th Georgia Calvary, which was assigned to Deering's brigade, in the division commanded by General William Henry Lee. On April 26th, 1865, General Johnston and General Sherman agreed to surrender terms, ending the war for nearly 90,000 soldiers in North Carolina, South Carolina, Georgia, and Florida, including J.C. Little who was in Greensboro, North Carolina at the time of the surrender.

In 1866, he became a clerk in a mercantile establishment in Louisville, Georgia. By 1869, he was running his own mercantile business and would become a prominent merchant in Jefferson County.

He married Mary Virginia Fleming of Columbus, Georgia in May 1872, and had four children together named William, Eunice, Edith, and Emma. Through this union, he became associates with Samuel Mathias Clark, who was married to Martha Helen Fleming, incorporating the Little & Clark

James Cain Little

Company in February 1904, with J.C. Little as President and Samuel as Vice-President.

According to Lucian Lamar Knight, founder and first director of the Georgia Archives, Louisville was the center of trade and political influence when it served as Georgia's capitol between 1796 and 1806. When the capitol moved to Milledgeville, combined with the lack of a railroad, progress and trading in Louisville stagnated. That was until 1879, when the Louisville & Wadley Railroad opened, a 10-mile railway connecting to the main stem of the Central of Georgia Railway.

J.C. Little entered the railway industry in 1879 when he became treasurer of the Louisville & Wadley Railroad, and later in 1888, would be President and Superintendent of the same railroad until his death.

A bedroom on the second floor of the home.

His wife Mary died on June 18, 1886, at the age of 32. He remarried in 1888 to Eleanor "Nellie" Patterson, and had four children together named Augustine, Malcolm, Robert, and Martha.

In 1875, J.C. Little bought half a city block in Louisville from William A. Wilkens, one of the earliest and largest property owners in Louisville at the time. There, he contracted L. J. Guilmartin & Co. to build his grand Gothic Revival-styled home. Featuring five bedrooms, two bathrooms, 15-foot ceilings, etched glass transoms over the interior doors, and a beautiful central staircase, the home was completed in 1876 at the cost of $4,000.

J.C. Little died on November 5th, 1917. During this time, Georgia's economy on a downturn as the boll weevil was destroying many of the crops in the state. Elizabeth P. Little, James' wife, never remarried and sold the house in 1924 to a C.W. Powers for $6,500.

The kitchen located in the back of the house.

As the economy fell even further during the Great Depression, the Home Owners' Loan Corporation foreclosed on C.W. Power's property. The Home Owners' Loan Corporation sold the property in 1943 to Minnie Willie McDaniel for $3,400.

In 1943, Home Owner's Loan Corporation sold the property to Minnie Willie McDaniel for $3400. In the years that followed, the property changed hands a couple times within the family until being sold to Eve Maria Willie Griffin in 1987.

During the 1950s, the house functioned as a boarding house and contained a beauty parlor on its right hand side. Author Ennis Willie, known for his influence on the crime genre, wrote his first book while living there. According to Ennis, he wrote the book in the first room on the left as you walk through the front door, typing it up on an old Royal typewriter that sat on the edge of a ping-pong table.

Opposite: The central staircase in the downstairs main hallway.

Dolls and stuffed animals lay on a couch and chair in the living room of the house.

Eve Maria Willie Griffin was a well-known lounge singer back in the 1960s and 70s, is Ennis Willie's sister and was one of the people who supported him in becoming an author.

Eve owned another residence in Augusta, Georgia and the house in Louisville was neglected. In 2017, the Downtown Development Authority of the City of Louisville took control of the home with the goal of stabilizing and saving the house. The Georgia Trust for Historic Preservation states that the home is endangered due to significant leaks in the roof. It is in need of a new roof along with repair of the water damage, electrical, plumbing and HVAC would need to be repaired and updated, and the exterior needs repairs and paint as well. The Downtown Development Authority patched the roof to temporarily halt any further deterioration but only time will tell what the house's fate is.

Opposite: Children's dolls were located throughout the house.

GREEN GABLES

William Twining Wells was born in Brooklyn, New York, on August 6th, 1854. He attended the School of Mines of Columbia University where he studied metallurgy.

W.T. Wells became well known as the inventor and developer of the Wells process of rustless iron and his subsequent company, the Wells Rustless Iron Co. Rustless iron is a form of wrought iron that has been chemically treated while in the furnace, coating the iron and preventing rust from developing. Rustless iron was advertised as being a suitable use for drinking water plumbing, due to its ability to prevent rust with both fresh and salt water. According to his obituary, W.T Wells manufactured this iron from his foundry in Little Ferry, New Jersey, with business offices in New Jersey. It also states that examples of his work can be seen at the Library of Congress in Washington D.C., as much of the trim was done with this process.

He later married Nora Stanford, and they had three children together. Nora was the eldest daughter of Senator Charles Stanford, and niece of Leland Stanford who founded Stanford University, was the Governor of California during the Civil War, United States senator of California, and President of the Southern Pacific Railroad and Central Pacific Railroad.

Nora had a tendency to get pneumonia, so the Wells family ventured to find a winter home in a much better climate for Nora's health. After traveling across the state of Florida, they chose Melbourne as the most desirable for its friendly residents, a number of outdoor activities, wonderful fishing along the river, and most importantly, an improvement in Nora's health. A property consisting of 150 acres was purchased and the Wells family began construction on their winter home, Green Gables, which was completed in 1896.

Constructed by Baker and Bell, Green Gables was initially designed in the American Foursquare-style and was modified multiple times throughout the years. It is rumored that the home was wired for electricity at the time of its construction, long before electricity was available in Melbourne, and powered with a generator driven by an artesian well.

The largest modifications to the home were done before 1910, and include probably its most notable feature, the octagonal tower and porch. The home was expanded to include a bathroom on the second floor between the two southern bedrooms. Another bathroom was added on the north side and the resulting space underneath was turned into a porch. These initial expansions were what turned the American Foursquare-style home into a Queen Anne-styled home.

The northern bathroom, added on sometime before 1910. A porch was built below this in the same style as the front porch.

There were many additions made to the house in later years, such as a laundry room and pantry near the kitchen. In the 1950s, a mother-in-law suite was added to the back of the house and the living room was expanded.

During his lifetime, W.T. Wells was one of the most prominent men in Melbourne not only due to his fortune, but due to his contributions to society.

When Green Gables was first constructed, it was isolated from the rest of the town and the only streets at the time were one of two blocks situated around the old Carleton Hotel. W.T. Wells decided to construct roads leading from his house in each direction and then donated them to the town.

There was no suitable school at the time either, so had one built known as Educational Hall and employed a Professor Winters from Deland, and invited other children in the town to attend the school as well.

The kitchen located at the back of the house. Back in the old days, the kitchen was usually situated in the back due to the heat that area of the house emitted.

One of the southern bedrooms. A bathroom was added before 1910 connecting this bedroom with the other southern bedroom.

Interest in Chautauqua was on the rise, a movement consisting of adult education events with speakers, teachers, musicians, entertainers, preachers, and specialists, with the first Chautauqua being held in the town church. As it grew, W.T. Wells allowed the use of the Educational Hall and later, built the town's first auditorium which could hold up to a thousand people and was described as having "perfect acoustics". W.T. Wells was the Vice-President of Chautauqua and became its President in 1907.

In the 1920s, he donated a 30 acre tract of land to the city of Melbourne for a park, now named Wells Park. Something to note, W.T. Wells also owned a pineapple plantation on the east side of the river, now known today as Wells Point. He also loaned money for the construction of the Melbourne Public Library and oversaw its construction.

His health began to decline until he passed away at Green Gables on July 6th, 1930 at the age of 75. Nora lived at there for another three years until her passing in October 1933.

The parlor room. You can see a pipe in the fireplace which was a later addition for central heating.

After Nora's death, their son Stanford Wells took up residence at Green Gables with his newlywed wife, Pearl Mitchell Lyman. Pearl's first husband, Louis, also died in 1933 with which she had three daughters, Lois, Gladys, and Katherine. After Stanford and pearl's deaths in 1971, their daughter Gladys would take up residence in the home. Throughout the years, it would continue to change hands between family members.

Currently owned by descendants of W.T. Wells, no one has occupied the home since 2004 when the house sustained severe damage during Hurricanes Frances and Jeanne.

Green Gables at Historic Riverview Inc. was formed in 2010 in hopes of preventing further deterioration of the home, protecting the home from demolition, and restoring the home to be used as a community event venue. Since their formation, they have repaired the roof, cleared overgrowth around the home, secured doors and windows, and treated the home for termites and other pests.

According to the floor plan, this was the dining room, though rather small.

In June 2014, the city of Melbourne issued a demolition permit allowing the owners to demolish the house. In April 2015, Green Gables at Historic Riverview Inc. struck a deal with the owners allowing them to purchase the home if they raised $800,000 by December 31, 2017, and preventing its destruction at least until then.

On May 18, 2016, Green Gables was added to the National Register of Historic Places.

By December 2017, the group had only raised $70,000 out of the $800,000 needed to purchase the home. As the deadline approached, the group was given an extension. Rather than paying $800,000, the group only needs to raise $275,000 by May 2018, when they will apply for a Florida Division of Historical Resources special category grant of up to $500,000. Hopefully by the time you are reading this, the home has been saved from demolition.

Opposite: The original staircase in the foyer.

THE FOAM DOME HOME

Nestled amongst the pine trees in a bamboo and fern filled forest near Santa Fe College in Gainesville, the dome house was envisioned, designed, and constructed by Mark Cohen in 1972, a landscape architecture student from the University of Florida. With pre-stressed welded rebar as the frame, polyurethane foam was sprayed on the exterior and a cement paint was sprayed in the interior of the home. The home was made up of two domes connected by an S-shaped hallway. The smaller dome contained 3 bedrooms and a bathroom, while the large dome contained another bedroom and bathroom, the kitchen, and living room with a sunken fireplace.

The dome was known by various names including the "Flintstones House", Hobbit House", Igloo House", but to the people who lived there, it became known as the "Foam Dome". In Mark's own words:

"The Foam Dome was coated with concrete on the exterior and a cement paint on the interior. The area around the sunken fireplace was brick. I had to prove to the county building inspectors that it wouldn't burn in order to get a certificate of occupancy. But, for the most part the county inspectors were very accommodating. They would send a different person out each time for inspections so everyone in the department had a chance to see it.

The foam dome home, now overgrown with vines, ferns, and pine trees.

I sprayed the foam on a few other dome frames of much smaller size for other owners but the technique just didn't take hold. I also sprayed store interiors and waterproofed tanks and roofs. Anything to stay in business until I could mass produce more foam domes. Eventually I shut down the company, sold the foam equipment, and got a job.

At the time of the construction of this dome home there was lots of talk about new types of construction and economical energy efficient homes. Does that remind us of the talk that's happening today? However, the timing wasn't right. Financing was hard to get for construction and for homeowners. Polyurethane had a bad name for its flammability and toxic gas when burning."

He lived in the home for seven years before selling it off to some friends of his. During those seven years, there were countless stories of parties filled with debauchery, which isn't surprising considering Gainesville is a college town. Mark Cohen would later pass away on December 26, 2015.

The living room. The old residents used to repaint the interior of the home every few years, like a space theme or a more nature theme as seen here.

The property would change hands multiple times throughout the years, even laying vacant for a number of those years, with many different people who would occupy the home.

One previous resident recounted their time there when they were living with a few other kids who also went to the University of Florida. They told of constant partying at the home, always for of pot smoke, kegs of beer, and psychedelic mushrooms which grew plentifully right down the road. The parties usually had upwards to 100 people, along with 30 more on top of the roof of the dome. There was even a 16-year-old kid who lived in the closet, often with his girlfriends, and paid just $100 a month for rent. On one notable occasion, one kid was blowing fireballs out of his mouth, 20 feet into the air from the roof.

Along with the parties, at one point some of the tenants thought it would be a good idea to grow marijuana inside of the home. Two of the bedrooms were filled, one-foot-deep, wall to wall, with dirt and after rigging the power meter, 8,000 watt

The hallway which connected the two domes of the house. Due to the materials and design of the home, it would probably be difficult and expensive to restore.

The bathroom located in between the two domes in the hallway. The shower looked incredibly uncomfortable for anyone over 6 feet tall.

The master bedroom which was only slightly larger than the other bedrooms and had its own bathroom.

lighting was also installed in the rooms. One evening after returning to class, a business card was found on the front door from a local detective saying "CALL ME ASAP", prompted them to shut down the grow operation. Despite that, the home was raided a few months later by police, accusing them of having a marijuana growing operation on the premises. After some searching, they only found small amounts of marijuana and dropped the case.

Eventually, the parties ended as the owner defaulted on their mortgage, returning the home to the bank. It has stood vacant for a number of years now and will stay vacant for the foreseeable future.

The house has been vacant ever since, changing hands quite a few times but you'll need a special lifestyle to live in a home as strange as this.

DUTTON HOUSE

The West Deland Residential District is a historic district in Deland, Florida, added to the National Register of Historic Places in 1992. The district is Deland oldest and most historic residential neighborhood with buildings dating back to 1884.

The John Dutton House is located here, a landmark of the historical district. Designed by Cairns & Fitchner, a local architectural firm, the Classical-Revival styled home is considered their greatest design.

Built in 1911, it was constructed under the supervision of local contractor Gus Lauman at a cost of $25,000, equivalent to about $630,000 today. The two-story wood framed mansion features Corinthian Columns which supported tiered verandas, ceramic tiles on the roof and gable ends, and scroll brackets, modillions, and dentils along the frieze.

John Wesley Dutton, a Georgia native, was a wealthy businessman who made his fortune running a naval store. At the turn of the century, his business controlled much of the turpentine and lumber harvest in the area. He began plans to build his mansion in 1908, when turpentine, lumber, and citrus were Central Florida's main industries. He lived here with his wife, Lilla Hart Dutton, and their seven children until 1921.

Front view of the Dutton House surrounded by a barbed wire fence with a sign out front promoting its eventual restoration.

In a letter written by Dorothy Douglass Dickey in May 1992, she explained how her and her family moved to Deland in 1918 and lived across the street from the College Arms Hotel, now the site of the College Arms Tower apartment building.

In 1921, she wrote that her father traded their house for the Dutton family home. It's not clear how long they lived in the house as she explains, "The last six years before I married my Stetson sweetheart, we lived in 7 states and 13 houses, three of which were in Deland. We left the end of July 1924."

Sometime after the Douglass family moved out, it became a funeral home known as the Griffith-Stith Funeral Parlor. In later years, it was converted into the Colonial Guest House which rented rooms out to visiting tourists. Last known as the Colonial Arms Apartments, the city condemned the building for numerous code violations.

A side room, possibly the sitting room. You can see the craftsmanship that went into building this house.

First Union Bank, now Wells Fargo, foreclosed on the property in 1990, and was put up for sale for $129,000. When no buyer could be found, First Union applied for a demolition permit in 1993 which was approved by the Deland City Commission. Just before its impending destruction, Peter Warrick, a publishing executive from Fort Lauderdale, purchased the home for $90,000.

With plans to restore the home, Warrick soon fell ill and asked the City of Deland to takeover restoration of the house. The City felt a non-profit organization would be a better fit for its restoration and in 1995, Historic Deland Inc. was established. The group was awarded several grants through the state which allowed restoration to resume.

By 2005, the organization's board of directors had diminished and a new board was established, in turn changing the name from Historic Deland Inc. to Dutton House Inc. After applying for more grants, restoration continued until 2008.

The grand staircase and foyer.

According to the organization's website:

"Although Dutton House Inc was approved for several State grants in 2008 because of the recession no historic restoration funding was allocated. We were allowed to reapply for 3 consecutive years all with the same results. By the time the State was once again allocating funds too much time had passed and our previous spent funds were now too old to use as matching funds for the grants.

Without matching funds we can't apply for new grants to continue restoration. We are actively seeking any and all possible avenues for matching funds. Unfortunately, we have not been successful to date. But we continue to try."

The group was able to complete the first phase of stabilization and 80% of the exterior was complete before funds diminished. After 25 years since restoration first began, the future of the mansion remains uncertain.

Opposite: The foyer. Notice the trimming on the ceiling.

ROOM #314, CARRIE'S APARTMENT

The six-story brick and limestone building was built in 1924 and opened as the upscale 310 West Church Street Apartments. Designed by architects Hal Hentz, Neel Reid and Rudolph Adler, the Georgian Revival styled building was built in the shape of an "H" which provided every room with a window while still able to house about 110 residents.

In 1944, the apartment building was converted into a hotel and renamed Three-Ten Hotel. Though it wouldn't be the last time it would be renamed as it would only be three years before it was renamed in 1947 as Hotel Southland, and again in 1949 to Griner Hotel. Finally, the hotel was renamed one final time in 1955 to the Ambassador Hotel, the name it is called by today.

As Jacksonville's downtown went into decline, the hotel fell into disrepair along with it. In 1983, it was added to the National Register of Historic Places, but code violations and multiple drug busts and raids have given the hotel a bad reputation and losing any hope of saving it. Most of the residents in the hotel at that time came from the adjacent LaVilla neighborhood, where most of the houses were condemned or demolished. Some of the homes were condemned due to drug raids by police.

On June 12, 1997, police raided the building after weeks of surveillance and undercover buys of crack cocaine. No drugs were recovered but two arrests were made and drug paraphernalia was found on the fifth floor. Police also found a hidden closed circuit monitoring system on the fifth floor, used to warn them of oncoming police or to monitor customers.

The Ambassador Hotel, as it was known as since 1955.

City property officials were with the officers during raid to check for safety-code violations and other problems. Among the code violations found were faulty wiring, cracked walls, improper screens, poor sanitation and lighting, and locked fire escape doors. Residents received notices stating that the building no longer complied with code and that they would have to be fixed to remain open. The hotel was officially condemned in 1998.

Since then, many people have been interested in renovating the dilapidated hotel, but as of yet, none of the plans have gone through. In 2005, renovations were halted at the hotel along with the nearby Duval County Courthouse. In 2009, Lamonte Carter, director of Oasis Venture Group, had plans to convert the hotel rooms into 50 apartment units but nothing has come of it.

Just recently in May 2011, Ryan Whitaker of Grandbridge Real Estate Capital, is seeking $6.25 million in debt financing and plans to have the apartments ready for leasing by Summer 2012. There has since been no work done to the building.

Mickey Mouse in a chef's hat is painted on the wall near the stove. An old resident said it was his uncle who painted that.

That's the history of the building which is readily available online. Since its opening though, there are hundreds of stories which haunt these halls which can only be told by the people who lived it. Photographing a place where someone once lived always seemed more personal to me, because you're essentially walking into someone's life. Or rather, the life they had. Nothing could prepare though when I walked into Room 314 of the Ambassador Hotel.

Room 314 was home to Carrie Bell White, Edward Green I and their three children, her history preserved on the walls of the small apartment. For 19 years, Carrie scrawled notes on the walls, from when she was born to doctor appointments to ramblings of a false accusation of a wrongful death.

According to Carrie herself, she was born on September 1, 1948, living away from her home until 1952 when she was returned to her parents in Jacksonville. On another walls, she writes, "I know my age 48 years old. Momma and Daddy won't tell me, they won't show birth certificates either, they said my

Some writing on the wall, left behind by Carrie Bell White who noted everything from appointments to the names of her family.

date of birth is correct." Nearby is a different birthdate, "August 23rd, 1948."

On another wall, she wrote, "I do not have a recorded birth certificate nor my son nor my husband we are Christians, American and black no Social Security # are correct either they are going to this years Assign us a social security card with our numbers on them and name Greene Edward I Greene Edward II Green Violet Mae."

"Mother to Infant female and 2 other Males All are Alive and Healthy Date of Birth December 12th, 1996 Live Birth, 6:00 a.m." Just above it, she writes, "2 Boys—1 infant girl from Edward Green I 1556 Fairfield Place I just recently gave birth to a 6 pound beautiful girl who look exactly like her paternal Father Edward Green I. Signed Carrie White" Written underneath is what looks like a social security number.

Fairfield Place is a street in the prominently African-American and impoverished East side of Jacksonville, and

1556 is a small wooden house built in 1943. Property records show that the property is owned by an Edward Green. The Fairfield address shows up again, alongside phrases such as "wrongful death" and "1976 baby ownly 6 years old falsely accused". The names of her husband and sons are listed here as well.

Wanting to find out the whole story behind these writings, I was able to locate a Carrie Belle White and a Carrie B. White, living in Jacksonville and attempted at contacting both of them via phone and through the mail. Unfortunately, my attempts at contacting either Edward Green or Carrie White deemed fruitless.

The rooms of the Ambassador are small and cramped, usually having more than four people sharing a room when it was still functioning.

EL JOBEAN GRAND HOTEL

Once part of Manatee County, the area located on the northeast bank of the Myakka River near Port Charlotte became part of DeSoto County in 1881, and in 1921 it became part of the newly formed Charlotte County.

In 1887, Daniel and Jane MacPherson from Scotland purchased 1071 acres of land at what was then known as Myakka Landing and planned out the town of Southland. Other than the establishment of a small fishing camp for sports fisherman, there was no development on the land and the property eventually went into receivership due to years of unpaid county taxes.

The Charlotte Harbor and Northern Railway extended its line to Southland in 1907, constructing a railway bridge over the Myakka River along with a small railway terminal.

In 1908, three men from Maryland bought the Southland property for its unpaid taxes. Years later, they resold the property to two men who constructed a turpentine distillery on the property in 1920, making turpentine a major industry for Charlotte County. The business though did not last long as the distillery went into foreclosure.

The entire 1071 acre tract of land that was Southland was sold to Joel Bean in 1923, sole owner of the Boston and Florida Realty Trust Company. The old Southland town plans

The front lobby, living room area.

discarded and were replaced with Bean's own plan for the new town of El Jobe-an, which he billed as the "City of Destiny".

The plan for El Jobe-an called for dividing the city into six wards, each with its own civic center border on a circular central plaza surrounded by a boulevard from which six thoroughfares radiated outwards in the shape of a hexagon. Six other streets would extend outwards from the central plaza and connect with the other wards. Lots bordering the central plazas were reserved for businesses and public buildings. There were also lots set aside within each ward for churches, schools, and recreational facilities. A casino, dance hall, and bathing pavilion was to be erected on the city's waterfront. Plans were also developed for a large modern railroad depot constructed in the center of town and an 18-hole golf course.

Joel Bean constructed the El Jobean Hotel, the Post Office and General Store and a small cottage he built for himself which doubled as a sale office, as a means to attract tourists and buyers to the new community he was developing. Bean

Much of the back portions of the building have collapsed or are on the verge
of collapsing.

wanted all of the buildings in El Jobean to be constructed in
the Mediterranean Revival style of architecture which was
popular in Florida during the 1920s land boom, and these
early buildings were to eventually be demolished.

The development was bound for success as Northern buyers
began purchasing lots, putting down modest down payments
and taking on large mortgages without even visiting the area.
Much of this was due to a land boom that had begun to gather
momentum in 1921. Spurred on by reports of large fortunes
made in Miami Beach by buying and reselling properties,
buyers sought out properties throughout the rest of the state of
Florida.

The land boom began losing momentum though around
1926 and finally came to a complete halt when the stock
market crashed in 1929. This forced landowners to abandon
the mortgages on their lots, and the Boston and Florida Realty
Trust Company folded as a result. Only early residents,
fisherman, and Joel Bean remained.

While the hotel mainly catered to fishermen, then called the Grand Hotel and Fishing Lodge, Joel Bean used it to house Metro-Goldwyn Mayer movie crews who came to El Jobean in 1931 to film Tarzan serials and a feature-length film starring Ann Sothern and Adolphe Menjou.

World War II improved the economy of the area when the Army Air Force Base, now the Punta Gorda Airport, was built in nearby Punta Gorda. The El Jobean Hotel continued to attract numerous customers, including entertainers and fisherman.

Joel Bean died in 1942 at the cottage he built in El Jobean. Neighbors took it upon themselves to start a collection to help pay for his funeral expenses.

After Joel Bean's death, the property was purchased by Leopold and Donna Simon, who were entertainers in various traveling circuses. The Simons spent their winters in El Jobean throughout the 1930s while on break from their performances, and purchased the property so they may continue to enjoy the area.

According to three public birth records, Leopold "Leo" Carl Simon was born on April 19, 1906 in San Antonio, Texas, though his death certificate and tombstone indicate he was born in 1905 which is an error. Per his two nieces, the family pronounced the surname Simon as "Sea-mon".

His parents, Leopold Simon (1866-1926) who was a pharmacist and drug store owner and Emilie Mueller Simon (1871-1947) were born and died in San Antonio, Texas. His only sibling, Elizabeth "Milly" Carolyn Simon Morris (1910-1964) married Patrick John Morris who had two daughters, Millicent and Nuala.

Opposite: The kitchen, located just adjacent to the front living area.

Inside one of the hotel rooms. The room was full of old records, Christmas decorations, and a wheelchair.

According to his two nieces, their uncle Leo who they referred to as "Polo", had red hair, blue eyes, and was born partially deaf. His was known as "Polo" to them because when first learning to talk as a child, their mother couldn't say Leopold and instead pronounced it as "Polo".

In the 1920s, he began working as a carpenter, and later as a construction foreman, where he worked on some of the most prominent commercial buildings in San Antonio. The San Antonio newspapers wrote about him once as being "a proficient high-board diver at the Brackenridge Park swimming pool".

Opposite: A bathroom which was shared among all the guests of the hotel.

Around the 1930s, he began his fire-diving act which involved him climbing a minimum 80-foot tall ladder, dousing himself in gasoline and setting himself on fire. He would then perform a swan, jack-knife or somersault dive into a 6-foot pool of water, which was also on fire. The pool was also surrounded by spikes that would have killed him instantly if he ever missed.

Later in life, he came up with a performance that he described as being much safer. The act consisted of him climbing into a small wooden box about the size of a casket along with three sticks of dynamite, lighting the dynamite with his cigar, and essentially blowing himself up.

He became known to many as Leo "Suicide" Simon, "Captain Leo 'Suicide' Simon", "Fire-Diver", the "Human Firecracker", and the "Dynamite Devil".

A photo which reads "Getting ready for it - Greetings, Leo Suicide Simon 5/6/1955" *Courtesy of Elizabeth A. "Bitsy" Gibson Wagner.*

In 1932, he married Donna Eslocker Simon, who always traveled together with Leo as he performed his daredevil stunts.

When the Simons purchased the El Jobean Hotel in 1942, their carnival lifestyle followed. A number of carnival and circus performers took up residence at the hotel during the winter months and later, made it their permanent home. Among these were the famous "Flying Wallendas" who would practice their high wire and trapeze acts behind the hotel.

The hotel operated until 1969 when the Simons retired due to Leo's failing health. He peacefully passed away in 1972 in El Jobean, and was buried at Gulf Pines Memorial Park in Englewood, Florida.

On September 29, 1999, The El Jobean Hotel was added to the U.S. National Register of Historic Places. It is one of two of the original buildings located in the old center of El Jobean. The cottage Bean lived in was destroyed by fire in 1991.

BIBLIOGRAPHY

Nash, Gary B. Forbidden Love. Henry Holt and Co., 1999

Andrews, Eliza Frances. The War-Time Journal of a Georgia Girl, 1864-1865. University of Nebraska Press, 1997

Roberts, L. Thomas. Deland. Arcadia Publishing, 2014

Pendleton, Edmund Monroe. Scientific Agriculture with Practical Deductions. A.S. Barnes & Company, 1875

Fleming, Walter Lynwood. The South in the Building of the Nation: Biography K-Z. Pelican Publishing, 2002

Herringshaw, Thomas William. Herringshaw's American Blue Book of Biography. American Publisher's Association, 1915

Busbey, T. Addison. The Biographical Directory of the Railway Officials of America. Railway Age Co., 1906

Candler, Allen D. Georgia: Comprising Sketches of Counties, Towns, Events, Institutions, and Persons Arranged in Cyclopedic Form. State Historical Association, 1906

Rozier, John. Black Boss: Political Revolution in a Georgia County. University of Georgia Press, 2012

Maki, Amos. Historic Ashlar Hall in Limbo After 'Renovation'. The Memphis Daily News, 2015

Norman, Bob. The Alien Has Landed. Miami New Times, 2006

Gleaves, Rebekah. An Interview with the Mongo. The Memphis Flyer, 2005

Copelon, Dianne. History Buff Saves Deland's Dutton House. Orlando Sentinel, 1993

Ivey, Tia Lynn. Historic Site in Madison in 'Peril'. Morgan County Citizen, 2017

Waters, Erika J and Blair. Tale of the Human Firecracker's Hotel. Messy Nessy, 2017

Pinkowski, Edward. Suicide Simon. Popular Mechanics, 1950

Rights Leader John McCown Crash Victim, Funeralized. Jet Magazine, 1976

Goodman Jr., George. N.A.A.C.P. is Assisting 11 Indicted in Georgia. New York Times, 1977

Campanella, Richard. A Gothic castle in Bywater? Ill-fated almshouse was once a New Orleans landmark. The Times-Picayune, 2016.

Veneziano, Heather. A Glimmer of Hope for Algiers' Touro Shakespeare Home. Preservation Resource of New Orleans, 2017.

Kaplan-Levenson, Laine. The WWII Internment Camp, 'Camp Algiers', Part I. WWNO New Orleans Public Radio, 2017

Kaplan-Levenson, Laine. 'Camp Algiers,' New Orleans' Forgotten WWII Internment Camp, Part II. WWNO New Orleans Public Radio, 2017

Paul Friedman, Max. Nazis and Good Neighbors: The United States Campaign against the Germans of Latin America in World War II. Cambridge University Press, 2005

Alexander-Bloch, Benjamin. The eerie, murderous past of St. Bernard's closed pet cemetery: Timetable. The Times-Picayune, 2014
Alexander-Bloch, Benjamin. Abandoned pet cemetery has eerie, murderous past. The Times-Picayune, 2012

Berman, Dave. Melbourne's Green Gables may go down in history. Florida Today, 2014

Neale, Rick. Green Gables added to National Register of Historic Places. Florida Today, 2016

Neale, Rick. Green Gables preservationists in race to raise $800,000. Florida Today, 2017

Neale, Rick. Green Gables organizers get critical fundraising extension to try to save Melbourne house. Florida Today, 2017

The City of Destiny. Florida Memory Blog, 2015.

REESE, Seaborn, (1846-1907). Biological Directory of the United States Congress, 2018

Judah Touro. Jewish Virtual Library, 2018

Brown, Brian. Birdsong-Hill-Elliot House. Vanishing North Georgia, 2014.

www.findagrave.com/memorial/89033598/leopold-carl-simon

www.georgiatrust.org/places-in-peril/foster-thomason-miller-house

www.georgiatrust.org/endangered-properties/little-house/

www.railga.com/louwarr.html

www.ftmhouse.com

www.madisonga.com

www.duttonhousedeland.com

www.savegreengables.org

www.abandonedfl.com

INDEX

ABOUT THE AUTHOR

David Bulit is a Hialeah native, a city within the Greater Miami area. He began urban exploring in 2009 after watching a documentary on it called 'Urban Explorers: Into the Darkness', and was fascinated with the stories and places, especially one portion of the film involving the exploration the abandoned Aerojet rocking testing facility near the Everglades National park.

He took up photography shortly afterwards to share with others the places he's visited, and has since had his work shared with both local and international newspapers and websites.

In 2015, he had his first book published titled "Lost Miami: Stories and Secrets Behind Magic City Ruins". More of his work can be found at www.davidbulit.com.

77934750R00077

Made in the USA
Middletown, DE
28 June 2018